my *heart*
is a stray bullet

my *heart*
is a stray bullet

kateri akiwenzie-damm

KEGEDONCE PRESS

R.R. #5 Wiarton
Cape Croker, Ontario
Canada N0H 2T0

The author gratefully acknowledges the financial assistance of the City of Ottawa,
Cultural Assistance Program in the original publication of this book.

Kegedonce Press gratefully acknowledges the financial support of the
Canada Council for the Arts.

Cover artwork by Rebecca Belmore.

Design and layout by Jerry Longboat.

Photograph of Kateri Damm by Tim Wickens, Ottawa.

KEGEDONCE PRESS
R. R. 5 Wiarton
Cape Croker, Ontario
NoH 2To
www.kegedonce.com

CANADIAN CATALOGUING IN PUBLICATION DATA

Akiwenzie-Damm, Kateri, 1965 -
My heart is a stray bullet/Kateri Akiwenzie-Damm.--2d ed.

Poems.
ISBN 0-9697120-9-x

I. Poetry. I. Title.

PS8557.A495M9 2002   C811'.54   C2002-903521-x

PR9199.3.A362M9 2002

CIP

Printed in Canada

for my niece and my nephew

Pietra Anna and Frederick Cullen Joseph Damm Holmes

and for

my grandfather

Joseph V. Akiwenzie
and my grandmothers
O. Irene Akiwenzie
and
Anna Damm
with love
always

Contents

In 1993, when this collection of poems was first released, I was living in Ottawa, finishing my Master's degree, and an active member of WINO, an Aboriginal writers group that got together regularly to read each other's work and share information on gigs, calls for submission, and other writerly news. The previous few years had brought major changes in my life. My Polish grandmother Anna Damm had died in December 1988. I was devastated. Then in 1991 my Anishnaabe grandfather died after a long illness. Although it was expected and we knew it was time to let him go, the reality of living without him was painful. We mourned and concentrated our attention on my grandmother. Secretly, I think we all feared losing her and hoped we could keep her with us if we held on tightly enough. However, less than 4 months later my grandmother died. They say it was a heart attack but I'm certain it was heartbreak over the loss of the man who was her companion and love for more than 50 years.

Shortly before her death, I visited my grandmother in the small local hospital in Wiarton, Ontario where she was being treated for her heart problems. We sat outside at a picnic table, talking and enjoying the summer day. Gramma asked me about my plans for the future, about marriage and family, and about returning to school. It wasn't until after her death that I realized it was her way to say goodbye.

The next time I saw her was at the wake. Though I'd rushed home from Ottawa I arrived at the hospital too late. She was gone.

My life changed dramatically at that point. To fulfill a promise to her, I applied to university. I quit the six month government job I was still doing almost four years later, moved from an apartment to a house, and made plans to take a trip overseas with a friend before starting back at university.

They say that when one door closes, another door opens. It's a cliché but I believe that my grandparents didn't leave without opening another door for me. In November 1991, I left for my trip to Aotearoa, knowing very little about the place or people but looking forward to meeting a few Maori writers with whom mutual friends had put my friend and me in touch. One of those people was Patricia Grace, a woman who would become my dear friend and whose family would become my "other family," my whanau. How we came to meet seems incredible to me — but I firmly believe it was a gift and that my grandparents somehow steered me in that direction.

The poems in my heart is a stray bullet were written over many years but most were written between 1987 and 1992. A few were written during the time of my grandparents' illnesses and deaths and they figure largely in the collection. Looking at the entire collection of poems now I see the roots of my life and my writing as well as the seeds of ideas and interests that have grown into the enduring passions of my life.

Looking back, the poem "desire" is the one that surprises me the most. I wrote it in 1992. I still wonder where it came from and how it came to be included in my book. The inspiration is not difficult to trace. I had a secret crush on a beautiful, married, Native man and the feelings he aroused in me inspired the poem but the poem wasn't really about him. I wanted him and fantasized about him. And I knew without doubt that I would never act on it. In fact, I barely knew him. So, I did the only thing I knew how to do to express and understand what was happening: I wrote a poem. The poem was unlike my other writing and sprang forth fully formed from a place inside me I didn't know existed. Or perhaps it was what I call "a gift poem" - a poem that arrives from somewhere outside of me and yet somehow is truly of me. Beyond that, I honestly don't know.

I do know I was not fully aware of the significance of the poem at the time. When I was putting together the poems for this collection, I included the poem "desire". At the time, I wouldn't have thought to call it 'erotic" and I was only vaguely aware that including it in the collection might be in any way daring. I believe now that I was able to be brave enough to include the poem precisely because I did not allow myself to think about what I was doing or why. If I had, I suspect I might have put the poem in a drawer, safely buried under a pile of other discarded poems and unfinished stories. Buried deep like my own desires were at the time.

Over the years since, erotica has become an increasingly important part of my development as a writer and as a person. More and more I have longed for images and stories of love between our people. Not the stereotypes and fantasies of Hollywood, sexually bored middle-aged North American housewives, nor those of men looking to affirm their virility and dominance; I wanted something true. If I was going to read fantasies about Aboriginal men, I wanted them to be like my fantasies, to stir my desire for flesh and blood Aboriginal men. I wanted them to be about love, not power. It was then I began to look for erotica by Indigenous writers. And slowly I began to write the love poems I longed for and was unable to find elsewhere. It was a creative and personal transformation that would "shake the earth" beneath my feet.

In retrospect it is also unbelievably fitting that the collection ends with the last poem I wrote before the book went to print: "from Turtle Island to Aotearoa." To me this poem represents a nexus, a point at which the people and places of my past and future came together. A pinnacle from which I can look back to see where I've come from and ahead to a then-unknown but foreseeable future. Little did I know at the time how important my connection with Aotearoa would become and how my work to create and strengthen international Indigenous alliances and collaborations would grow increasingly important in all aspects of my life both professional and personal. Little did I know then in how many ways the tree would indeed "bear fruit on many branches."

In 1993 I dedicated my heart is a stray bullet to my niece Pietra, my nephew Freddie, and my grandparents Anna, Joe and Irene. Since then my family has grown. I now have another beautiful little niece and nephew, my brother's children Samantha Anna Damm and Adam Damm. It is my dream that they find the land, people, and poetry that surrounds them an enduring source of joy, comfort, and inspiration.

I would also like to thank the many friends who have shared my life since this collection was first published, especially the two men who taught me about love, loss, forgiveness, and letting go, and to the friends and lovers who will share my future. Chi megwetch.

May we all grow in love and beauty.

Kateri Akiwenzie-Damm
Neyaashiinigming, Cape Croker Reserve
September 2002

wilderness

wilderness poem # 1

eyes lowered body bent forward
move slowly with care
through this wilderness that is my love
then when you leave there will only be
echoes of your sounds
a barely discernible path
and a few ashes from your fire
swirling in the wind
like a warning
then the wilderness will remain
untamed as it should be
and you will emerge
with clean hands
and the will to survive

woman to woman

(woman)
your body is ignited
not cold
like mine
but smooth as polished wood
stretched tight skin
like night over sky
a fire dance
sustaining
an instrument
no
alive
an animal
sleek
untamed
unaffected

                                    (woman)
                        i am a young woman
                    body coiled tight as a spring
                        a gathering of cells
                            and memory
                        a stream of blood
                        banked on a shore
                        of fine bone china
                                and
                            scraped clean
                    my skull still keeps its secrets

                            i am a maker
            my fingers clutch steel instruments
                and soft-pounded skins
                to make a jacket for you
                                see
                    see how my hands move
                            see how
            i make people and clothe them all
                        touch them
                they are not afraid to be held

sturgeon

i twist and gasp
open and close my mouth
searching for air
whenever a sturgeon is caught in the rainy river
i know
the feel of strange hands touching my body
the struggle
to be free
the longing
to go where i want to go
i feel
the impact of stick or rock on bone
the splash of colour
then the emptiness that is my head
my head like a midnight sky if the stars and moon were captured
by another heaven
i know
even when i am awake again
sitting at the kitchen table
staring at my plate with its bramble design
and rough chipped edges
i know

that is why i do not eat sturgeon
because i know
when a sturgeon is caught in the rainy river
i am a sturgeon
and i dangle on hooks

to you who would wage war against me

i

there are many lines
you have not traced on my palms
still
you think you know me

when i speak
you nod knowingly
as if
you've already read my mind
and are only politely acknowledging
the confirmation of my spoken words

ii

but you cannot possibly know
what i've been contemplating
these days

my head is full of blood
but you show no fear
and i do not trust my hands
they look to me like stones

you do not cower when i approach
though i feel like a runaway train
and i can hear your voice cool and steady
while my brain screams profanities
into the air around your ears

our past has given you no reason
to be afraid
but still i am surprised you cannot see
the danger burning brightly in my eyes
the fire i am struggling to control

iii

as i sit stewing in the kitchen's false light
with tears my daughter
comes to me
frightened by what she cannot see
afraid tonight to sleep

i hold her in my arms
singing soft words of comfort
feeling her heart quickly
beating against my chest
knowing before i can think that
i have forgiven us
for our stupid little wars

knowing in that incandescent light
that anger will never move me
as delicately as she has moved me
this night

words for winter

i cannot touch you
but i know how you dream
about a country
where snow falls in sacred secret places

i picture you
standing out
against the whiteness
tall
breathing life into the air around you
while the world rushes headlong

i sigh
cloaking myself in the darkness of a january night
watching the snow fly
safe from the howling storm outside

"is that fair?"
i don't know and can only guess
that this marginal shelter
is like a memory of some earlier life
some future history
(where survival dwells)
or maybe it is some maternal longing
that cannot be expressed
except in dreams
that no one else can read

"are you afraid to fall in love love?"
the connection between love and life
tonight is tenous
this place is too much like a land of long shadows
cast by fleeting figures i do not taste or touch or smell
i climb the tower freely
but perhaps i am too unfeeling
or dizzy from this height

"will canada go to war?"
the question is thrown from mouths
as though we have all returned to babel
and cannot speak our own languages
as though we have been forced to speak words we cannot understand

the sky lies flat
so can we talk about tomorrow
or live on toast and tea
while men kill men?

the answers are
waiting
on the tip of my tongue

my secret tongue and ears

i

as dusk falls from this autumn day
(like a blood red leaf)
the darkness whirls madly to the earth
carried by windfury

still
i sit alone
against the lamp's dim light
staring at the hieroglyphics in my skin
thinking
if i could simply read these symbols
tell my own story to myself
and know i had spoken a truth
but these lines mean nothing to me
except a number of years gone by
and a certain lack of understanding
so
sadly as the day flies
the truth remains
a secret i keep from myself

ii
in a second of silence
raindrops pellet
the roof and walls
echoing off
the tin and glass and brick
like a verbal assault
that i cannot say i understand
though i would cross a sterile desert
or stand naked in a december snow
to gain that wisdom

iii
so another day passes unceremoniously
while i sit like a fool
in this easy chair
the stars shining above
(like asterisks to some important note)
tempting us to close our eyes and forget the rhetoric of hate
that was spoken
moments before
in the space
between us

iv
but
i cannot let sleep steal away
my secret tongue and ears

in the darkness
of my house
i seek
perfect vision clarity
within my own deaf silence
i strain to hear
syllables unspoken

v
and still i don't understand
the intricate design
of raindrops rolling down my face at dawn
or the map of my vision against my skull
still
i have not learned the language of my quest

even as sunrays sneak past shadows
and i wake in a shower of falling stars and your
light caress
still
i have no words to say

you are my suicidal tendency

i can hardly believe
the way the deep blue sky surrounded the bone bare tree limbs
that knocked against each other in the sun
the same way we knock against each other
in these small rooms

was it only yesterday
before the sun hit
the eastern side of our sky
that i wounded myself
to prove the depth of my skin
(have you ever noticed the sun when it is a blood red song of war)

did you know
i have sung a thousand songs to your mood swings
written a thousand poems of the echoes
without finding the words you won't be able to forget
even after a thousand thousand suns have kissed this tongue
of sky

so do you even care
that you are my suicidal tendency
do you even care
that i rumble through the dry grass of august
to lay under the stars at night
because i can't bear to sit in the cold light of silence
between us

i can't even lie to myself
and say
you don't matter to me
the truth is like a mirror i haven't been able to turn away from
though i can't even see myself anymore

truth is
i can't see the lines separating us
truth is
it's scary

one night i dreamt
that when the sun shone on my heart i dissolved
into the lines on your face

and you smiled

stray bullets
(oka re/vision)

my touch is a history book
full of lies and half-forgotten truths
written by others
who hold the pens
and power

my heart is a stray bullet
ricocheting in an empty room

my head was sold
for the first shiny trinket
offered

my beliefs were bought cheap
like magic potions at a travelling road show
with promises
everyone wants to believe
but only a fool invests in

my name was stolen
by bandits in black robes
my world was taken
for a putting green

i witness

i witness

i will give you my testimonies
and i will bear the brunt of your questions
and disbelief
i will offer my photographs as evidence
and describe the captured moments
with expert accuracy
i will disconnect my heart

                and

                          my head

for the moment
to show you what it is
you want to know

i will be there when the case is heard

being from cape croker

i am of a people who live between two bluffs
a not unlikely place
for any anishnaabe

howdy partner

i knew a little mixedblood girl
who used to tell people
she was

"part cowboy"

and

"part Indian"

(i used to think that was funny)

indian enough

i have felt the sting of accusation
from non-Natives who say i am "not Native enough"

i have been told countless times
i "don't look Indian"

i have been encouraged to forget
rise above
leave behind:
destroy my
self

i have seen the disappointed looks
at my fair skin shining
natural blond streaks of hair glistening
and not even a feather
buckskin
or jingle dress
to redeem me

i have read the dismay on tightly held faces
when i speak in complete English sentences
none of which begin "many moons ago"
none of which are spoken in telltale sing-song speech pattern
expected from a "Native speaker"

as i speak
i have felt a cold martyred patience
blasting from those who want to hear "Native storytelling"
for as long as the words shall flow

　　　to them i am not "colourful" enough in reality

and I have been told
by a Native woman
an elder
that I am "not a very good Indian"
because I can't speak Ojibway

I have been held suspect

because I have endured with no noticeable scars
(and even some success)
in the "White" school system

because working with the federal government
was interpreted as a change in loyalties
(though I struggled there too for being too outspoken
to know my place)

because I have lived most of my life in cities
on quiet tree lined streets

because my skin pales in comparison

because I am a C-31 Indian

i have felt myself splinter into pieces

im/potent/ial

between the lines

               i ricochet from position

                                      to position

   dangerous
   in my need
  to find a niche

                      unable to stop

afraid

   of impact

      caught static

     in

        mid

           air

time after time
after
time

      concepts   smack   WALLS OF REALITY
                 into

and in between
i am a potential threat and
or impotent

           impact
            of
        body and mind

                                    i am

mixed blood: notes from a split personality

There is no denying that postsecondary education erects barriers between...
marginalized students and their families and cultures. That recognition is sad but
necessary. If you identify with these communities of concern, you might feel torn in two
by your education, feel as if your loyalties are constantly being divided as you learn....
  --Kathleen Martindale, Susan Shea and Lana Major

1. (divisions)

i am having an out of body experience
as i sit in this chrome and plastic chair
i can hear the wood veneer of this table
crying like an abused child
i can feel part of my spirit
swirling around my head and
i am dizzy with speed
and light
ness
while the other part of me
concentrates wildly
all power
in this pen
in the voices of women around me
in staying rooted in my place
while the tornado whirls
a film in front of my eyes
till i am dulled beyond
belief

2. (bloodTies)

i need
to remember
my grandfather's hands
the lines and smoothness like a rock
wearing years
the knuckles swollen with arthritis
and a lifetime of toil on the land
veins pulsing beneath the surface

i need to remember
my grandmothers' hands
moving
always moving

i need to remember
gramma's soft and spotted hands
tender
wielding words with precision
without craftiness

i need to remember
gaga's stirring, mixing hands
straining
in the well-stocked kitchens
of toronto's money-rich
and later
in her own small kitchen
mixing cookie dough while us kids waited
impatiently

yes i need to remember the blood
mingling freely in me

i need to remember
the strength of
bloodlines

(3. (reunion invocation)

heal me
of this strange blood dis/ease
re/pair this compass
so i can find my way with startlingly clear directions
stitch my skin together with strong threads
and i will be like patchwork: fragmented but whole

heal me)

i lose track of the land

at night there are no voices
singing me gently to sleep
though i know they whisper
outside these strange walls

i look to the sky
for the sweet light of stars
but night is never dark here

i long to join the dance of the earth
- i knew the movements once

i dream of the wind
the damp smell of earth
and the footsteps of animals
dancing by moonlight

my body is tired and aching

blood rushes to my feet
drains into the pavement
is pulled through my scalp

i lose track of the land

what the earth might say

what the earth might say

there is no true silence
everything every bird and blade of grass
calls out its story as it must
and though you may see nothing
even the empty places are filled with meaning
respect too the spaces
inside them another language speaks
but to learn it you must listen
for tongues once stolen
now sing the wisdom of your saints
so listen like a forest
sometimes love and hate cry out
beyond the range of your ordinary hearing
so shrug off the coils that separate you
put off the veil that covers your soul
take the scales from your eyes
see and hear like a true human

names

somedays
      when i hear lawnmowers up and down the street
      and children's voices drifting in the wind
as i pull weeds
i think
i want to quit tending my names
and see what might grow
wild and obscure in their place

and other days
      when i am driving home
      on the road that takes me through toronto
            past exits i have taken before
            to visit friend and relations
      or when i remember picking strawberries in the early morning
      with my grandparents and cousins
            and i recall the taste of berry juice on my lips
            and the feel of the berries between my fingertips
      or when i am searching for morels at cape
            surrounded by the smell of cedar
      and a twig snaps beneath my feet
i bear in mind
that now as ever
even the wilderness needs protection and thanks

and then once more
i say my names slowly
with care

april recollection

our breaths mingled with sun and air
while we stood witness
to the day the seasons collided
so beautifully
and with so much sorrow
our hearts shook like branches in a storm

we alone were the trembling
we together watched
papa's long last journey
as an eagle traced his tribute overhead
with wings pounding a steady pulse
joining the rhythm of the earth
and our own heartbeats
as one

now a perfect cycle
moves us to this moment
that blooms bittersweet
with memories of this man
we mourn and remember
but like bears waking
in the warmth of spring
we leave our empty caves
to stand proud upon the land
breathing testaments of love that never ends

so today we hear our voices
that once seemed only to sing our sadness
strengthened with the echo of his voice
becoming his life-song celebration

my grandmothers

anna   irene
there are so many memories
shaping   your words
     my image of you
        my love for you
     my history of us   are a life line
my life
in toronto i remember
eating the chocolate bars that marked every visit
and shopping in eaton's bargain basement
     trying to keep up   i cling to
to
     you   like i would cling to your warm hands
and i remember you
telling the butcher on eglinton
i was your granddaughter   when i was a child walking with you to church
and how straight and smiling you stood
     and how shy and secretly proud i was
i remember being with you
in your "bachelor" apartment on bloor street
when i first realized i was woman   and you had a way of speaking
i remember   so words would hook in my brain
your voice awakening me
with the eerie
pain full cries that snuck out in the dark
from that secret secure place you held them
     in the daylight

                                                    and even now
i remember buying you five star brandy
and the thanksgiving mom jo-anna you and i
went rummaging through flea markets
where you bought me a pink rhinestone pin
for two dollars
then
when we had dinner
i remember
how you had too much wine
and when i think
of how we all laughed together   i can feel your gentle tug
then i remember you
so relaxed and smiling
i remember massaging your feet
in the hospital and watching the heart
monitor jump when you laughed and told jokes
i remember too how much i took you for granted
i remember my ears burning from listening
        while you recounted your days
and how many times i wasn't really listening   at the other end
because i thought i'd heard it all before
and was young enough to believe i'd always remember it
        now this is all i can say   of my thoughts

familiar cartography

so my grandmother arrived in this country
a young woman
already with secret thorns in her heart
that twisted
until that december day the hospital phoned
to say she was leaving for good

immigrant woman
carting a basket full of sorrow
across an ocean
creating alone a new life
with sturdy hands
private dreams
and strong will

later
raising a son
with no family to share the griefs and celebrations
no mother to share secrets
or to pat her hand and tell her everything would be fine
while sipping cups of tea and lemon
on those long nights the boy was too scared to sleep
and she had to rise early next morning
to ready him for school
before facing the day full of cooking and cleaning
that stretched across her horizon

so grandmother
this is part of what i know
and still i cannot map your life here
your arrivals and departures
the elevations of the streets you walked
the colours of earth you touched
remain unknown
at least by me
along with many aspects of your life
whole chunks of years like puzzle pieces
are missing
and since you left
i have lost more pieces than i have found

so sometimes i wonder
if anyone ever really knew you
and i stare across an empty kitchen table
as the day unfolds

the book you left:
in memory

(i.)

grandmother you gave me a book of flint and feather
yet how little i know
about you
or the woman whose words you left me

(ii. both)

that you both wrote poetry and had dreams
that much i know
that in you the blood of saints and spirits mingled
        and could not be ashamed of who you were
that headbands and beads were signs
        proclaiming that you would not renounce your heart
        or forget where your feet took stand:
that much i know

(iii. subVersion: going fishing)

that you could use a costume like bait
to reel people in to your line of thinking
        while your stories and smiles gutted their lies
            and filled their thick heads with new stars
        so quickly so quietly
            they left
            smugly unaware of the change
                    or of how you threw the little minds back unaltered
                        with the hope that they would grow
: oh that much i know

(iv. building)
and that you tried to build a bridge
        by piling words like stones
            one by one by one:
yes that much i know

(v. contender/conTender)

but of the struggles you fought
        to walk a path between two worlds
            while finding forgiveness for those who would push you off the edges
and of the scars you carried from those who would muzzle you
        as you tried to find a voice that could not be forgotten
or of the secret places you took shelter
        when the storm clouds gathered:
of all that i know too little

(vi. disTRUST and DISbelief)

of the self doubts and hope
of the twisted ropes of loyalty
and the bone crunching betrayals
the redemptions exemptions and passions:
of that too i know so little

(vii. i)

so here am i
searching for solace and the whisper of your breathing

(viii. (or 4 x 2))

in the words you left between my ears and the edge of creation
in the poetry you etched in field notes and small memories
in the songs you left hidden in tall trees and the rhymes you uncovered in streams

in this book you left to me

a familiar archeology
for rebecca

together will we walk the bruce trail in early spring
when mud will assert the margin of the land
and i will show you places of my childhood

will we watch the ghosts of children
running through the leaves
or will we drink tea from broken china cups
buried and unearthed near the roots of trees

will we sit on the edge of jones' bluff
daring each other closer
while the wind fills our ears and
will we grow afraid for each other

will we hear our grandmothers' voices calling
and will we instantly run towards them
will we emerge together from that place
and will we go back again

will we walk down the hill picking up stories
and bits of broken glass
will we give each other stones
then stomp our rubber boots against the pavement
just to hear the sounds and feel alive

will we live a day sitting at my kitchen table
drinking tea from broken china cups
and will we talk till the sun comes up
and still have more to say

will we grow our hair grey and walk familiar places
when our legs are cold and stiff
and will we still see the ghosts of children
running through the leaves
then will we be there for the burials
promising each other we'll never be alone
and after all
will we sit together near the roots of trees
drinking tea from broken china cups

searching for true words
for greg

another cycle has spiralled us further out into the galaxy
another growing season slumbers
while we sift through words like bakers with flour
like these pages are snowcovered distant fields
and we are setting our prints upon them
as if breaking trail

as if breathlessly
as if bending into the wind
as if dreaming of august

our pace quickens

but there are no footprints visible now
and as we move we lose sight of each other
snowblind
we call out
hands outstretched
searching
protective tentative
connected

(though each of us knows
there is no "we"
between two people

are there still no true words
for two people moving together
on different paths?)

river song

take me down to the river's edge with a rush of tears and the sound of angels' wings
give me breath with a host of desire and a single touch lifted from despair
wash my fears at the martyrs' grave with the blood of saints shouting holy names
sing my pain in mid-summer rain with forgotten words and a tongue of fire
dance my heart like a laughing child like a drunken man with sallow cheeks lash
my burdens to another cart with ropes of your hair and no mercy feed my head
with beauty and stories collected like shells from old women in kerchiefs
and storm whipped beaches forget my ugliness and the imperfections large
and small that make me ashamed but human carve my name in the dead of night
beyond all stars and forgiveness

desire

desire

i want you
inside me
i want to be
inside you

i want your love
your babies
your breath rhythm
against my cheek

i want skin touching
my name on your tongue
i want to shake the earth
with you

i will be

i will be your refuge on howling december nights
when it is too cold to be alone
and there is no screaming against the wind
i will be your blanket under stars
and cover you till dawn
my body soft yielding against your pain
i will be your rainy day raven
hanging by your door with stories
and the sound of laughter in my throat
i will be your underground madonna
gathering children to my arms
never showing signs of anger or defeat
i will be your lonesome whistle call
marking time and empty hours
wandering like a dream
i will be your honour song
celebrating your survival
tossing your name into infinity
i will be your fist of stone
to pound away all sorrow and regret
to grind fate into submission and pulverize all tears
i will be your act of contrition
to make you whole
and pure beneath the sun
i will be your salvation
the ground of your creation newly-sprung
confession of your cruel frailty
i will be your monument to living
striking out against dust
and the brief domain of memory

lovers' psalm

if love had no name
    i'd give it yours
    then i'd whisper love's name in the morning without fear
if love lost its faith
    i'd show it your poetry
    i'd let it hold your hand until hope stretched across the city's sleeping gutter dwellers
if love lay bleeding on the soft moss-covered earth
    i'd gently place it in your arms
    i'd promise it your kiss at daybreak
if love grew afraid to wander ancient riverways
    i'd show it your body
    i'd let it worship you like a lost man adores a map
if love lost its voice in a blizzard
    i'd heal its throat with your laughter
    i'd tell it stories of your living until it could speak
if love lost its mercy through years of abuse at my hands
    i'd reform it with your memory and the feel of your skin
    i'd throw its anger beneath your feet like a crushed serpent's head

the resurrection of desire

the craft of devotion
is the passion of saints idiots lovers
and abusers of every kind
those whose heads of filled reflections and suffering
float slowly downstream
while their lips move as if in prayer
counting branches waving from the shore

homeless
forgotten sailors
swept in a tidal wave of their own creation
destroyers of flesh
worshippers of forever
mapping the way to heaven
across feet and hands and heads and torsos
rejecting the beautiful mortifications that haunt the minds of perverts
the guilt of sinners three scalps hanging from their belts
starkly insanely lovely

delicate in flight these wingless birds
transform into sweet bloody joyous messiahs
noiselessly stripping themselves of flesh
to the envy of those who sing of pain and make love in the dark

manitouwan oh manitouwan
earthy earthly exalted exiles
where is the raven
or those strange ancient monsters of the waterways
who would drag an innocent to that other world
where death sleeps

tell us
what ceremony or madness will safeguard their return?

alternatives: one two three

i.   **indian giver**
you are alone giving gifts
to the talking rocks
knowing your lover would not understand
and the neighbours would cluck and circle like hens
yet here you are
having found your way in pickups
and on paths your feet remembered
when your thoughts were lost
the stars   a hollow in your gut   and
biting autumn winds followed
bringing a clarity that made you cry
and again you were humble

ii.   **indian soul food**
you are pouring tea
into mugs stained with use
as the old woman your grandmother speaks
and you listen without defense
to her words and worries
while your friends drown this same saturday night
at a roadside six miles away
and your grandmother feeds you bannock
of her delicate hands and instinct
and she says your name into the universe
with a smile
while love dances around the table
then suddenly you are the moon and air and trees

iii.   **indian ink**
you are telling tales
about a trickster with two faces
who was always going backwards
when he was moving forwards
and the children giggle and poke each other
unaware of the chief who waits
to meet the handshakers at indian affairs
before flying back home empty handed
but you know
you know
only that the story you tell
is alive and laughter
echoes forever

poem without end #3

nanabush is an english professor
sitting in an ivory tower
looking down upon the masses who go herd-like to their classes
writing books that no one looks at
reading poetry on money
drinking tea and eating crumpets with the dead men who turn women into bone

nanabush is a landlord who turns off the heat in winter
and a tenant who throws parties while the babies are fast sleeping
the one who keeps you laughing even when your heart is breaking
and the one who tells you stories when it's wisdom you've been seeking

nanabush is a singer
she's a heavy metal drummer
she cheats and swears and talks of death
then lets you meet her children
she throws pearls onto Parliament Hill
dresses men in clothes of sheepskin
then she sits alone and drinks cheap wine and cries into the table
while she prays for gods' forgiveness because she can't forget the sabbath
she's a lonely wooden goddess on a path into damnation

nanabush knows jesus
he plays tricks on paul and peter
he unlocks the gates and steals a peek
and cannot keep the secret
he will shit in darkened hallways
pull your pants down to your ankles
he will take your love and steal your life
and give you dreams and laughter

nanabush is a trapper who wears sealskin pajamas
he eats fish that have been poisoned
speaks a language now forgotten
and when he jumps into the river
half crazy with survival
he tries to touch the bottom to create a new religion
but he floats up to the surface
and his hands are cold and empty
so the animals give him shelter because they know the winter's coming
and when he wakes they wait together for the storm that is approaching

silent nearly frozen they turn into a monument of stone

kegedonce

i thought about you all last night
now here you are
when my eyes are cloudy
and my tongue is swollen
giving me words as if tomorrow depends on them
you say
nniichkiwenh this morning i heard a bird's voice calling to the sun
and i was that bird
i was a swallow swooping into forest
then i was that forest turning my leaves towards the warmth and light
i say nothing
then you sing me your swallow song until my words are loosened
and come pouring out like a dammed river bursting in spring
i say
words are heavy with meaning
they are the true survivors
echoing into infinity when we have become bones cradled by the earth
you say
we belong to them and they belong to us
i say to you
words are my manitouwan my conjurors
with their magic the spider can be set in her web
the old people can live in the memory of generations
people from every direction can be made kin
the world can be recreated out of a fistful of clay
then
i pour my words over you smoothly
you give your words to me in song
i throw my words like poisoned arrows
but you steal the venom and give me back to myself
together we are healed with words
so we open our ears and take the scales from our eyes
letting our words shine like silver in the sun
together we are different yet one
speaking a language of true people
then you say in my voice
we are joined to each other as we are joined to this land
and i say in your tongue
i do not know how we came to this spot
but maybe it is enough to know that we are here
we are safe
and we are together

from turtle island to aotearoa

(i – new arrival)

morning shatters
like ice in our lungs
shallow breaths hanging ragged
above our heads
the tent is swimming
as women men children
twist turn
in a joyous rush to feed together
nniichkiwenh and i emerge slowly
from our cocoons
spinning in transformation
but unlike the caterpillar
we carry hope in our dull heads
as we shake off our old selves
to join the waves of maori
lapping at the shore of the marae

(ii – answering a call)

yesterday
the convoy that was mataatua waka
led us eastward to this place
where i finally come to understand
being called from home by voices i do not recognize
(but perhaps my true ears heard them
carried on the wind
or my true eyes read them in driftwood
like messages in a bottle)
and now i am aware
of slow cautious steps taken
inside this gate
where songs of family lines are cast
like nets across a sea of faces

(iii - drifting)

my moccasins step timid
on this part of mother earth
waiting for the pounding of other like-covered feet
my ears swivel but cannot hear the spirits whispering
"so this is what it is to be
a stranger in another land" i think to myself as foot follows foot

but feeling the pull of my ancestors
i am like someone walking against the current

while all the while
my head drifts slowly home
where i know the bending of the trees
and the sounds of undeveloped places
where my sister's children dream
and my grandparents' bones are cradled by ahki
where the lost spirits roam
and the heartbeat echoes
where my words are
(buried under rocks hidden in snow drifts
resting in flower beds
floating on clear bay waters
filling the forest)

here i am the quiet one
here i must reach across an ocean to find the right words

(iv - gathering stones)

once more under the moon
and the words of these people
do not jangle like jagged rocks in my head
the steady rhythmic pounding of voices
is wearing the sounds smooth
so that now the strength of the tide is apparent
even to one who stays close to the shore

tomorrow aotearoa will be waiting
with more gifts
and new stones to harvest
but tonight with only my own hollow thoughts for company
sleep overtakes me
carries to the place of dreams
every echoing sight and sound and smell

(v - an awakening)

the morning sky breaks
i wake
stretching into a new day
that yawns before me like a mother's child
i wake
peel off my blanket shell
to air so cool and gray
i retract and re-cover
listening as bits of conversation tell me
the house is awake

i am still
but my thoughts are bats in a cave
settling in dark corners of the room
as i sink deeper into the pillow
like a footprint in the sand

weeks from now
i will fall through the sky to turtle island
clutching a bit of papatuanuku in my fist
i will create a new beginning for myself
on the solid back of canada

(vi - long-distance connection)

now the day hangs directly overhead
and my sister's voice is sap running in my veins
though our words are nothing more than
leaves falling from sturdy limbs

feet firmly planted
i call for my sister's daughter
who pours out the drops of knowledge
she has gathered to share with me
so that suddenly i am a woman drinking under arid midday sun
thus revived i offer stories to her safe-keeping
showering with love the signs of new growth
later we are all embraced
by the child's grandmother my mother
who grows more and more like her mother before her

"everyone is fine" she says

the roots are well protected

(vii - actionsong)

far into another aotearoa night
stories are told so the young ones will remember
in turn
i make simple gifts of gathered words
but if i could sing
i would sing songs of thanks
to all our relations who guide our steps
to the whakapapa whispered on the waves
to the tangata whenua who have not challenged my being here
or my attempts at poetry
to the earth winds sky water
to moon stars and sun
to creatures of land and air and sea

if i could dance my actions would say
what my voice cannot

(beginning)

now this i know:
tomorrow will bring another day of remembering and forgetting
already clouds are gathering
calling each other closer
tomorrow more rain will fall
and someday our union
will bear fruit on many branches

yes
maaba anishnaabe on aotearoa
maaba rain on fertile soil
maaba the tree of all trees
so the story goes

KATERI AKIWENZIE-DAMM

is a band member of the Chippewas of Nawash, Cape Croker Reserve on Georgian Bay, Ontario and is of mixed Ojibway/Polish Canadian/Pottawotami/English ancestry. She was born in Toronto where she lived for several years before her family moved to the Cape Croker area in 1976. She received her Honours B. A. in English literature at York University in 1987 and her Master's degree in English literature from the University of Ottawa in 1996. She has lived at Neyaashiinigmiing, Cape Croker Reserve since 1994. *my heart is a stray bullet* is her first collection of poetry.

REBECCA BELMORE

is an Ojibway woman from the town of Upsala in Northern Ontario. She is renowned for her work as both a visual artist and performance artist. As a performance artist, Ms. Belmore has collaborated with many other Native artists at clubs and galleries around Canada. Ms. Belmore's visual art has been shown in galleries across Canada and the U.S. and was featured in "Land, Spirit, Power" at the National Gallery in Ottawa.

megwetch

Great thanks to those who supported in various ways the original writing and production of this book: Rebecca Belmore, Doug Chomyn, the City of Ottawa, fellow WINO members Anne Acco, Allen DeLeary, Tony (Joseph) Dandurand and Armand G. Ruffo.

I would also like to say chi megwetch to those who have assisted with the production of this edition: Renee Abram, Jerry P. Longboat, and the Kegedonce 'family'. A sincere thank you to the many Indigenous writers who have encouraged, inspired, challenged, and supported me over the years. Special thanks to: Patricia Grace, Joy Harjo, Haunani-Kay Trask, Basil Johnston, Maria Campbell, Joseph Bruchac, Richard Van Camp, and Dean Hapeta. Thanks also to the Canada Council for the Arts for supporting the work of Kegedonce Press.

As always, love and thanks to my family and to the home land for giving me a place to stand.

KEGEDONCE PRESS
R.R. #5 Wiarton, Ontario
Canada N0H 2T0
www.kegedonce.com